NO LONGER A SLAVE

Establishing Your Identity in Christ

GBENGA SHOWUNMI

NO LONGER A SLAVE
Establishing Your Identity in Christ

Copyright ©2026 by Gbenga Showunmi

Paperback ISBN: 978-1-965593-76-9

All rights reserved. No part of this publication may be reproduced, distributed, or transmitted in any form or by any means, including photocopying, recording, or other electronic or mechanical methods without the prior written permission of the author except in the case of brief quotations embodied in reviews and certain other non-commercial uses permitted by copyright law.

Published by Cornerstone Publishing

A Division of Cornerstone Creativity Group LLC
Info@thecornerstonepublishers.com
www.thecornerstonepublishers.com

Author's Contact

To book the author to speak at your next event or to order bulk copies of this book, please, use the information below:
pastorshow@gmail.com

Printed in the United States of America.

DEDICATION

This book is dedicated to the **Destinystar family**, a people I am honored and privileged to pastor. You have embraced truth with humility, faith, and a genuine hunger for God, allowing His Word to shape not just what you believe, but how you live.

My prayer is that these pages help establish your identity in Christ, strengthen your confidence, and deepen your freedom. Thank you for walking this journey of faith together. It is a joy to serve and grow with you.

Pastor Gbenga Showunmi

Galatians 4:7 (NKJV)

"Therefore you are no longer a slave but a son, and if a son, then an heir of God through Christ."

CONTENTS

DEDICATION iii

INTRODUCTION vi

PREFACE ix

1. Saved But Still Thinking Otherwise 1

2. How Religion Trains Powerlessness 9

3. The Psychology Of Spiritual Slavery 19

4. Sonship Consciousness 29

5. Covenant Thinking 37

6. Expectation As A Spiritual Law 43

7. Confidence Without Arrogance 49

8. Faith That Speaks First 55

9. Peace As Proof Of Trust 63

10. Thinking Like An Heir Every Day 73

CONCLUSION 82

INTRODUCTION

One of the greatest discoveries of my walk with God is this simple truth: many believers are not defeated by the devil, they are limited by their thinking.

Over the years, I have watched sincere Christians pray with passion, serve faithfully, and love God deeply, yet struggle with fear, inconsistency, and quiet frustration. They know the Scriptures. They believe the promises. Still, something inside them hesitates. Something pulls them back. Something whispers, "Maybe this is not for you."

That something is not always demonic. Many times, it is a mindset that was never healed.

When I wrote *Understanding Your Inheritance*, my assignment was to open the eyes of believers to what belongs to them in Christ. I wanted God's people to see that salvation did not only rescue them from sin, but restored them into a family, a covenant, and a supernatural heritage. That message remains true and vital.

But revelation alone does not always produce manifestation.

I have learned that you can know what belongs to you and still not live in it. You can quote promises you secretly feel unworthy to experience. You can believe God loves you and still approach Him like a stranger. You can be an heir in Christ and still think like a slave.

This book was born out of that burden.

The Holy Spirit began to deal with me about the **inner battles believers fight quietly**. Not battles with witches or demons, but battles with fear, inferiority, scarcity thinking, and spiritual intimidation. These battles do not always show on the outside, but they shape how far a believer can go.

God does not entrust authority to minds still shaped by slavery.

This is why many people desire power but struggle with peace. They want dominion but live anxious. They ask for boldness but still feel small on the inside. Until the mind is renewed, the life cannot rise.

The inheritance God gives us is real. It is complete. It is secure. But how we **see ourselves** determines how much of it we can walk in.

This book is not written to condemn you. It is written to free you.

It is written to help you identify thoughts that are not aligned with your new birth. To expose religious patterns that sound spiritual but train powerlessness. To restore the consciousness of sonship so that faith flows naturally, not forcefully.

You cannot enforce outwardly what you have not settled inwardly.

Before you can truly **occupy**, you must first **think like an heir**.

My prayer as you read this book is simple: that the Holy Spirit will gently but firmly realign how you see God, how you see yourself, and how you respond to life. That something heavy will lift from your heart. That confidence will replace intimidation. That peace will become normal again.

PREFACE

This book was born out of pastoral moments. Conversations after service. Quiet prayers with people who love God deeply but still feel restrained on the inside. Over time, a pattern became clear. Many believers are genuinely saved, committed to Christ, and faithful in practice, yet they live cautiously, manage expectations, and struggle to rest in who they are. Their faith is real, but fear still speaks too loudly.

No Longer a Slave was written to address that inner conflict. Not to accuse. Not to rush anyone forward. But to walk patiently through the process of establishing identity in Christ. This book is not about striving harder or proving faith. It is about alignment. About allowing truth to settle deeply enough to change how you think, how you wait, how you speak, and how you live each day.

As you read, take your time. Let the Holy Spirit highlight what needs healing and affirm what He has already established. Freedom grows best where the heart feels safe. My prayer is simple. That as you journey through these pages, fear will loosen its grip, confidence will rise quietly, and peace will become a familiar companion. You are no longer a slave. You are learning how to live from what Christ has already secured.

Gbenga Showunmi

CHAPTER ONE

SAVED BUT STILL THINKING OTHERWISE

There is a quiet tension that many believers live with but rarely name out loud. It is the tension between what they believe to be true about God and how they actually relate to Him in everyday life. They are genuinely saved. They have encountered Christ. They worship, pray, serve, and sincerely desire to please God. Yet beneath that sincere devotion, something remains unsettled. Their faith feels careful. Their prayers feel measured. Their expectations feel restrained. They belong to God, but they do not feel secure in His presence.

They know they are forgiven, yet they approach God cautiously, as though forgiveness might be fragile. They know they are loved, yet they brace themselves for disappointment. They know the language of inheritance, yet internally they still live as though access must be earned. This disconnect creates an inner strain that is difficult to explain. On the outside, everything appears faithful. On the inside, freedom feels incomplete. This is not because salvation failed or because Christ's work was insufficient. It is because thinking has not caught up with redemption.

Jesus spoke plainly when He said, *"If the Son makes you free, you shall be free indeed"* (John 8:36, NKJV). His words leave no room for partial freedom. What He secures is real, complete, and irreversible. And yet Scripture also reveals something sobering. A person can be truly free in Christ and still struggle to live free if their inner world remains shaped by fear, survival, and old patterns of thinking. Chains can be broken while the habits of captivity linger. Freedom can be granted while the mind still lives cautiously, as though captivity is only one mistake away.

Salvation is Complete, But Renewal is a Process

When a person comes to Christ, something decisive happens immediately. Salvation is not a gradual unfolding; it is a spiritual event. The sinner is justified, the broken are reconciled, and the old identity is replaced with a new one. Paul says it without hesitation: *"If anyone is in Christ, he is a new creation; old things have passed away; behold, all things have become new"* (2 Corinthians 5:17, NKJV). This newness is not symbolic language or emotional optimism. It is an objective spiritual reality established by God Himself.

At the same time, Scripture is clear that while the spirit is regenerated instantly, the mind often lags behind. Years of learned fear, religious pressure, survival thinking, and distorted expectations do not dissolve overnight. That is why Paul exhorts believers, not unbelievers, to undergo transformation through the renewing of the mind (Romans 12:2). A person can belong fully to Christ and still think in ways that reflect their former captivity. Until the mind is renewed, the spirit may know God as Father while the thoughts still expect a master. The heart reaches for intimacy, but the inner voice whispers caution. This inner contradiction creates tension, and it is within that tension that slavery thinking quietly survives.

Slavery Is Bondage, Not Biblical Servanthood

One reason slavery thinking persists is because it is often confused with faithfulness. Scripture honors servanthood deeply. Moses served God. David served God. Paul called himself a servant of Christ. In each case, servanthood is voluntary, relational, and rooted in love and devotion. Servanthood flows from relationship, not fear.

Slavery, however, is something entirely different. Slavery is obedience driven by fear rather than love. It is compliance rooted in self-protection rather than trust. It is the posture of someone who believes acceptance must be maintained and punishment is always close. That is why Paul draws such a sharp distinction when he writes, *"You did not receive the spirit of bondage again to fear, but you received the Spirit of adoption by whom we cry out, 'Abba, Father'"* (Romans 8:15, NKJV). Paul does not say believers were delivered from serving God. He says they were delivered from bondage. The opposite of bondage is not independence or rebellion. It is adoption. Adoption replaces fear with belonging and uncertainty with security.

Fear Reveals a Slave Mentality

Fear becomes one of the clearest indicators that slavery thinking is still active beneath the surface. The writer of Hebrews explains that Christ came to release those who lived their entire lives subject to bondage because of fear (Hebrews 2:14–15). Fear keeps believers guarded. It teaches them to obey carefully rather than confidently. A slave obeys because disobedience feels dangerous. A son obeys because relationship feels secure.

John reinforces this truth when he writes, *"There is no fear in love; but perfect love casts out fear, because fear involves torment"* (1 John 4:18, NKJV). Fear torments because it never allows the heart to rest. It assumes punishment, rejection, or withdrawal is always near. When fear dominates a believer's walk with God, it is often not because of rebellion, but because the mind is still interpreting relationship through captivity rather than sonship.

When Slavery Thinking Sounds Spiritual

One of the most deceptive aspects of slavery thinking is that it often hides behind spiritual language. Phrases like, "I don't want to bother God," "I'm just waiting to see if God really wants this," or "I'm not sure I qualify," sound humble on the surface. Yet humility is not insecurity. True humility rests in truth. False humility hides behind fear.

That is why Scripture invites believers to approach God boldly. *"Let us therefore come boldly to the throne of grace"* (Hebrews 4:16, NKJV). Boldness here is not arrogance. It is confidence rooted in access. Slaves keep their distance. Sons draw near because they know they are welcome.

The Older Brother: Faithful Yet Bound

Jesus illustrated slavery thinking vividly in the parable of the prodigal son. While the younger son's rebellion is obvious, the older son's bondage is subtle and deeply familiar. He never left home. He worked faithfully. He obeyed consistently. Yet when joy entered the house, his heart resisted it. His words exposed his mindset: *"All these years I've been serving you… yet you never gave me…"* (Luke 15:29, NKJV). He lived in the house, but thought like an employee. He measured relationship by labor and reward by effort. He never felt entitled to joy.

The father's response exposes the tragedy: *"Son, you are always with me, and all that I have is yours"* (Luke 15:31, NKJV). The problem was never access. It was awareness. Many believers live in God's house with full access, yet slavery thinking prevents them from enjoying what already belongs to them.

From Earning to Inheriting

Slavery thinking always tries to earn what God has already given. It confuses faithfulness with qualification. Yet Scripture is unambiguous: *"If children, then heirs"* (Romans 8:17, NKJV). Inheritance is not earned. It is received. Paul explains that an heir can live like a slave if maturity and understanding have not developed (Galatians 4:1). Legal status does not automatically produce lived confidence.

This is why so many believers are weary, not because they disobey God, but because they obey Him from fear. Their obedience is heavy because it is driven by pressure rather than rest. Jesus addressed this directly when He said His yoke is easy and His burden is light (Matthew 11:29–30). Fear-driven obedience drains the soul. Love-driven obedience strengthens it.

Standing Fast in Freedom

Scripture makes God's intention unmistakable: *"Stand fast therefore in the liberty by which Christ has made us free"* (Galatians 5:1, NKJV). Freedom must be guarded mentally. Bondage thinking can return if the mind is left unattended. You are not trying to become free. You were freed at salvation. What remains is learning how to **think free**.

So pause for a moment and reflect honestly. Do you approach God with confidence or caution? Do you pray expecting love or bracing for disappointment? Do you believe God delights in you, or merely tolerates you?

These questions are not meant to condemn. They are meant to invite healing.

You are not a slave trying to earn freedom. You are a son learning how to live free. And that journey begins in the mind.

CHAPTER TWO

HOW RELIGION TRAINS POWERLESSNESS

When Devotion Exists But Power is Absent

One of the most subtle enemies of spiritual freedom is not open sin, obvious temptation, or even persecution from the world. It is religion without relationship. This kind of religion often looks holy, disciplined, and respectable, yet quietly trains believers to live powerless lives. It rarely announces itself as harmful. Instead, it cloaks itself in spiritual language, routines, and expectations that feel normal, even commendable.

This subject is difficult for many people because religion is often confused with devotion. Many sincere believers were introduced to God through religious environments. They learned how to attend church, respect Scripture, obey rules, and avoid visible wrongdoing. None of those things are inherently wrong. The danger emerges when religious practice replaces relational intimacy, when duty substitutes for delight, and when fear quietly becomes the motivator behind obedience.

Jesus Himself confronted religious systems more than He confronted sinners. This was not because religion is always evil, but because it becomes dangerous when it replaces relationship. Religion can teach obedience without freedom. It can promote reverence without confidence. It can encourage discipline while silently reinforcing fear. And when fear becomes the foundation of one's walk with God, slavery thinking is strengthened rather than healed.

Religion Without Revelation Produces Distance

At its core, religion is humanity's attempt to relate to God without revelation. It relies heavily on external behavior, structured routines, and moral compliance while often neglecting the condition of the heart. When revelation is absent, intimacy suffers. God is approached as an authority to be managed rather than a Father to be known.

The Apostle Paul addressed this problem directly

when he warned of people who maintain spiritual appearances while lacking spiritual substance, describing them as *"having a form of godliness but denying its power"* (2 Timothy 3:5, NKJV). Paul did not criticize the form itself. He confronted the absence of power. Religion without revelation may produce discipline, but it cannot produce transformation. It may regulate behavior, but it does not renew the mind or heal the heart.

Revelation, by contrast, draws people closer to God. It replaces fear with understanding and duty with desire. It reveals not only what God requires, but who He is. Where revelation is present, intimacy grows. Where revelation is absent, religion fills the gap. And religion, when left unchecked, often trains people to approach God as slaves rather than sons.

When Rules Replace Relationship

One of the clearest signs of religious conditioning is an excessive focus on rules without relational context. Rules themselves are not the problem. God gave commandments. God established principles. Boundaries matter. But rules were never designed to replace relationship. They were meant to flow from it.

Jesus rebuked the Pharisees sharply for this very imbalance, saying, *"You cleanse the outside of the cup and dish, but inside they are full of extortion and self-indulgence"* (Matthew 23:25, NKJV). Their lives were outwardly impressive, but inwardly disconnected. Their obedience was meticulous, yet mechanical. It was driven by fear of failure rather than love for God.

Religion teaches people to ask, "Did I do enough?" Relationship teaches people to ask, "Am I walking with Him?"

The first question produces anxiety because it never has a clear answer. The second produces peace because it rests on presence rather than performance. When rules dominate without relationship, believers may appear disciplined while quietly feeling distant, unsure, and internally restrained.

How Fear Becomes a Training Tool

One of the most damaging aspects of unhealthy religion is how easily fear becomes its primary motivator. Fear of judgment. Fear of displeasing God. Fear of missing His will. Fear of being disqualified or rejected. Over time, this fear shapes how believers think, pray, and obey.

While the fear of the Lord is biblical and rooted in reverence, fear-based religion distorts this truth into intimidation. Scripture tells us that *"the fear of the Lord is the beginning of wisdom"* (Proverbs 9:10, NKJV), but wisdom is not terror. Reverence draws us closer to God. Terror pushes us away from Him.

John makes this distinction unmistakable when he writes, *"There is no fear in love; but perfect love casts out fear, because fear involves torment"* (1 John 4:18, NKJV). Fear produces torment, not transformation. Religion that relies on fear trains believers to obey God while never feeling safe with Him. Over time, this erodes confidence. People follow rules but struggle to exercise authority. They avoid sin but hesitate to pray boldly. They believe God hears prayers, yet remain unsure of their own standing.

The Pharisees: Religious Yet Powerless

The Pharisees represent one of the clearest biblical examples of how religion can coexist with powerlessness. They fasted regularly, prayed publicly, tithed meticulously, memorized Scripture, and enforced moral standards rigorously. Yet Jesus repeatedly exposed their spiritual emptiness.

He said to them, *"You search the Scriptures, for in them you think you have eternal life; and these are they which testify of Me. But you are not willing to come to Me that you may have life"* (John 5:39–40, NKJV). They knew the Word but missed the Person. They possessed information without intimacy. Knowledge without relationship produces either pride or fear, but never power.

Jesus did not withhold power from them arbitrarily. Their mindset prevented them from receiving it. Religion trained them to manage appearances, not cultivate intimacy. And without intimacy, authority remains inaccessible.

Performance Without Identity

Religion often defines people by what they do rather than who they are. Over time, believers begin to measure spiritual health by activity instead of intimacy. How often they pray. How long they fast. How consistently they serve. While spiritual disciplines are valuable, they were never meant to replace identity.

When identity is unsettled, disciplines become burdens rather than tools. Paul warned the Galatian believers about this danger when he asked, *"Having begun in the Spirit, are you now being made perfect by the flesh?"* (Galatians 3:3, NKJV). Religion subtly pushes believers back into self-effort. Sonship calls believers to live from grace.

How Powerlessness Is Inherited

Religious powerlessness is often passed down unintentionally. Many believers learned how to relate to God from environments shaped more by fear than intimacy. They were taught to obey God, but not to trust Him deeply. They were warned about judgment, but rarely assured of love.

Over time, this produces believers who are sincere but unsure. Faithful but hesitant. Disciplined but inwardly restrained. Jesus addressed this generational burden when He said, *"They bind heavy burdens, hard to bear, and lay them on men's shoulders"* (Matthew 23:4, NKJV). Religion places expectations on people without providing the grace to sustain them.

Grace Restores Power

The gospel is not the removal of God's standards. It is the restoration of power to live according to God's will. John captures this beautifully when he writes, *"The law was given through Moses, but grace and truth came through Jesus Christ"* (John 1:17, NKJV). Grace does not lower God's expectations. It empowers obedience. It restores confidence. It dismantles slavery thinking.

Where religion says, "Try harder," grace says, "Come closer." Where religion produces fear, grace produces faith Where religion restrains, grace releases.

From Fear to Relationship

God never intended His children to live afraid of Him. Scripture emphasizes access, closeness, and confidence repeatedly. Paul writes, *"In whom we have boldness and access with confidence through faith in Him"* (Ephesians 3:12, NKJV). Boldness here is not arrogance. It is the settled assurance of relationship.

Religion teaches distance. Sonship teaches access. Slaves keep their heads down. Sons lift their eyes.

A Pastoral Word

If your walk with God has been shaped more by fear than love, more by duty than delight, more by pressure than peace, this chapter is not meant to shame you. It is meant to free you. Religion may have trained you, but revelation can renew you. God is not looking for frightened followers. He is raising confident sons and daughters who know Him and trust Him.

Before we talk about authority, dominion, and occupation, we must dismantle the religious structures that keep believers small on the inside. Power flows most freely through hearts that feel safe with God.

The next chapter will explore how slavery thinking affects the inner life, emotions, and self-perception of believers, and how the Holy Spirit begins the work of inner healing.

For now, let this Scripture anchor your heart:

"Now the Lord is the Spirit; and where the Spirit of the Lord is, there is liberty" (2 Corinthians 3:17, NKJV).

Religion may restrain.
Grace releases.
You were not saved to live powerless.
You were redeemed to live free.

CHAPTER THREE

THE PSYCHOLOGY OF SPIRITUAL SLAVERY

Spiritual slavery rarely begins with demons, curses, or external opposition. Those realities exist, but they are not usually the starting point. Bondage begins much more quietly, and far more subtly, in the mind. Long before a believer struggles outwardly, something has already settled inwardly. A way of interpreting life has taken root. A narrative has formed about God, about self, and about what is possible. Expectations have been shaped not by truth alone, but by experience, disappointment, fear, and repetition.

This is why Scripture places such weight on the mind. The enemy understands something many believers underestimate. You do not need to imprison a person physically if you can keep them bound mentally. If the mind is restrained, the life will follow. If the inner world is conditioned toward fear and limitation, outward freedom will always feel risky and unfamiliar.

This chapter is not about psychology in the secular sense. It is about the inner mechanics of spiritual bondage. It is about how slavery thinking develops, how it expresses itself internally, and how the Word of God dismantles it over time. Until believers understand how bondage operates in the mind, they may love God sincerely and still live beneath their inheritance without knowing why.

Bondage Lives in Patterns, Not Just Moments

One of the most dangerous misconceptions about spiritual bondage is the belief that it is always dramatic. Many assume bondage looks like overt sin, addiction, rebellion, or visible failure. While those can be expressions of bondage, Scripture reveals that slavery often hides in patterns of thought rather than public behavior.

The book of Proverbs states it plainly: *"For as he thinks in his heart, so is he"* (Proverbs 23:7, NKJV). Notice the emphasis. Not as he prays publicly. Not as he confesses Scripture. Not as he behaves in front of others. As he thinks in his heart. The inner world eventually shapes the outer life.

Bondage thinking forms gradually. Fear becomes familiar. Insecurity becomes normal. Condemnation becomes expected. Over time, the mind learns to anticipate limitation. It prepares for disappointment rather than breakthrough. It assumes rejection before connection. Eventually, the believer begins to live defensively rather than expectantly. Faith may still be present, but it is restrained. Hope exists, but it is cautious. That is the psychology of slavery. It does not scream. It whispers consistently until limitation feels wise.

How Spiritual Slavery is Learned

No one is born again with slavery thinking. It is learned. It is acquired through experience, environment, and interpretation. It is often shaped by rejection, unanswered questions, disappointment, and sometimes well-meaning but fear-driven spiritual instruction. Slavery thinking is reinforced when hardship is interpreted as divine displeasure rather than spiritual formation. It deepens when correction is received without reassurance of love.

Israel's journey out of Egypt illustrates this process vividly. God delivered them with undeniable power. He sent plagues. He parted the Red Sea. He defeated Pharaoh publicly and decisively. Their freedom was not ambiguous. It was unmistakable. Yet shortly after their deliverance, when pressure arose, their thinking revealed what still lived inside them.

They said, *"Because there were no graves in Egypt, have you taken us away to die in the wilderness?"* (Exodus 14:11, NKJV). This was not a theological statement. It was a psychological one. Fear had hijacked perception. Later, they said, *"It would have been better for us to serve the Egyptians than that we should die in the wilderness"* (Exodus 14:12, NKJV).

That statement reveals the psychology of slavery. Bondage thinking prefers familiar captivity over unfamiliar freedom. Even when captivity is painful, it feels predictable. Freedom, by contrast, feels exposed. Slavery thinking clings to what it knows, even when what it knows is limiting.

When Slavery Thinking Distorts Perception

One of the most damaging effects of spiritual slavery is distorted perception. Bondage thinking does not see reality clearly. It filters everything through fear. Challenges appear larger than they are. Identity appears smaller than it truly is.

When Israel stood at the edge of the Promised Land, twelve spies saw the same land. They observed the same terrain, the same cities, and the same people. Yet they returned with radically different conclusions. Ten spies responded from fear. Two responded from faith.

The ten said, *"We are not able to go up against the people, for they are stronger than we… We were like grasshoppers in our own sight"* (Numbers 13:31–33, NKJV). Notice where the problem began. Not with the giants. Not with the land. But with how they saw themselves.

Slavery thinking always exaggerates opposition and minimizes identity. It trains the mind to interpret challenges as confirmation of inadequacy rather than invitations to trust God. It assumes difficulty means disqualification. Faith, by contrast, interprets difficulty as the context where God's power is revealed.

The Inner Voice That Sustains Bondage

Every mindset has a voice. Slavery thinking speaks quietly but persistently. It does not shout. It reasons. It sounds sensible. It often disguises itself as wisdom.

"You're not ready yet."
"Others are more qualified."
"Don't expect too much."
"Be realistic."
"You should be grateful for what you already have."

These statements sound mature. They sound cautious. But they quietly undermine faith. They teach believers to manage life rather than expect transformation. They encourage survival rather than inheritance.

Scripture invites believers to a different posture entirely. Paul declares, *"Now to Him who is able to do exceedingly abundantly above all that we ask or think, according to the power that works in us"* (Ephesians 3:20, NKJV). Slavery thinking sets ceilings. Faith removes them. Slavery prepares for disappointment. Faith prepares for God.

Condemnation: The Fuel of Slavery Thinking

Another powerful psychological pillar of spiritual slavery is condemnation. Condemnation is not the same as conviction. Conviction draws a believer toward repentance and restoration. Condemnation pushes them toward shame, hiding, and self-rejection.

Paul addresses this clearly when he writes, *"There is therefore now no condemnation to those who are in Christ Jesus"* (Romans 8:1, NKJV). Yet many believers live as though condemnation is still active. They replay past failures. They revisit old mistakes. They measure themselves by who they used to be rather than who they are now.

Condemnation trains the mind to stay small. It convinces believers they must always compensate for their past. But Scripture declares, *"If anyone is in Christ, he is a new creation"* (2 Corinthians 5:17, NKJV). New creation means new beginning. Slavery thinking refuses to let the past stay buried. Sonship insists it has been crucified.

Why Slavery Thinking Resists Authority

Authority requires confidence. Slavery thinking resists authority because it is uncomfortable with confidence. It associates boldness with danger and humility with invisibility. It teaches believers that staying small is safer than standing firm.

Yet Jesus said plainly, *"Behold, I give you the authority… over all the power of the enemy"* (Luke 10:19, NKJV). Authority was given, not earned. But authority must be received mentally before it can be exercised practically.

Many believers know authority exists doctrinally, yet hesitate to walk in it. Something inside still feels unqualified. That hesitation is not humility. It is bondage thinking. Authority flows most freely through minds that are secure in relationship.

How the Holy Spirit Rewires the Mind

Freedom from spiritual slavery is not achieved through positive thinking or self-improvement. It comes through truth. Jesus said, *"You shall know the truth, and the truth shall make you free"* (John 8:32, NKJV). Freedom is the result of revelation replacing lies.

The Holy Spirit guides believers into truth, not merely information. Paul describes this process when he writes, *"We all, with unveiled face, beholding as in a mirror the glory of the Lord, are being transformed"* (2 Corinthians 3:18, NKJV). Transformation happens as perception changes. As truth reshapes interpretation. As identity replaces fear.

A Gentle Moment of Reflection

Many believers are harder on themselves than God ever is. They remember failure more vividly than grace. They recall correction more readily than redemption. Let me ask you gently: What story do you tell yourself when you fall short? What voice speaks loudest when you pray? What do you expect God to say when you approach Him?

Your answers are not accusations. They are indicators. They reveal whether slavery thinking still has influence.

From Mental Bondage to Renewed Thinking

The journey out of spiritual slavery is not instant, but it is intentional. It requires awareness, truth, and patience with yourself. Paul reminds us that thoughts must be confronted and brought into alignment with Christ (2 Corinthians 10:5). Freedom is not pretending fear does not exist. It is refusing to let fear define reality.

This chapter is not meant to leave you introspective. It is meant to prepare you for restoration. In the next chapter, we will begin establishing **Sonship Consciousness**, where identity replaces insecurity and belonging replaces fear.

For now, let this truth settle deeply in your heart:

"Where the Spirit of the Lord is, there is liberty" (2 Corinthians 3:17, NKJV).

You are not broken.
You are being renewed.
Slavery thinking may have shaped your past, but it does not define your future.

CHAPTER FOUR

SONSHIP CONSCIOUSNESS

Freedom does not begin with authority. It begins with identity. Many believers long to walk in bold faith, spiritual authority, and confident obedience, yet find themselves hesitant, restrained, or inconsistent. They want to exercise authority in prayer, stand firmly against opposition, and live with assurance before God, but something inside feels unsettled. The reason is often simple but deeply rooted. They are attempting to operate from power without first settling who they are.

In the Kingdom of God, identity always precedes assignment. Authority flows naturally from belonging. Until sonship is established in the heart, authority will feel forced and confidence will feel unnatural. People may attempt bold actions outwardly, but inwardly they remain unsure. Faith feels like effort instead of expression. Courage feels like strain instead of rest. This chapter is about restoring sonship consciousness, not as a doctrine to agree with, but as a reality to live from. Sonship is not something believers perform. It is something they awaken to.

Christianity itself is not first a system of beliefs or a code of conduct. It is an invitation into a family. At the center of the gospel is not merely forgiveness of sins, but adoption into relationship. God did not simply cancel a debt. He welcomed sons and daughters home. The Apostle John captures this wonder when he writes, *"Behold what manner of love the Father has bestowed on us, that we should be called children of God"* (1 John 3:1, NKJV). This is not poetic exaggeration. It is theological reality. Salvation does not merely make us followers of God. It makes us His children.

Paul reinforces this truth without qualification when he declares, *"For you are all sons of God through faith in Christ Jesus"* (Galatians 3:26, NKJV). Sonship is not reserved for spiritual elites. It is not a reward for maturity or longevity. It is a gift received at salvation. Yet many believers live as though sonship is something they must grow into, rather than something they are meant to grow from. When sonship is postponed mentally, believers relate to God as though acceptance is conditional and belonging is fragile. They obey, but they do not rest. They serve, but they do not feel secure. Sonship consciousness restores the foundation.

Living From Acceptance, Not Approval

Sonship consciousness is the settled awareness that you belong to God, that you are accepted by Him, and that your place in His family is secure. It is the quiet confidence that you are not tolerated, but loved. Not managed, but embraced. Not on probation, but at home. This consciousness reshapes the inner world. It affects how believers pray, how they respond to correction, how they interpret delay, and how they handle failure. Sonship does not deny growth or responsibility. It anchors both in relationship.

Jesus modeled this consciousness perfectly. Before He performed a miracle, before He preached publicly, before He confronted demons or religious systems, the Father spoke over Him, *"You are My beloved Son, in whom I am well pleased"* (Luke 3:22, NKJV). The timing matters. Jesus had not yet done anything publicly. The Father affirmed identity before assignment. God establishes who you are before revealing what you are called to do. When identity is settled first, assignment becomes an expression, not a burden.

This distinction becomes clear in how approval is understood. A slave works to gain approval. A son works from acceptance. Slavery thinking is driven by the question, "Have I done enough?" Sonship asks a diffcrent question, "What is my Father doing, and how can I join Him?" Paul explains this shift when he writes, *"When the fullness of the time had come, God sent forth His Son… to redeem those who were under the law, that we might receive the adoption as sons"* (Galatians 4:4–5, NKJV). Adoption changes posture. It removes fear-driven striving and replaces it with relational obedience.

When acceptance is settled, obedience becomes willing rather than anxious. Faithfulness flows from love, not fear of rejection. The heart is no longer negotiating for approval. It is responding to relationship.

The Spirit Makes Sonship Real

Sonship is not only a theological truth to be affirmed. It is a spiritual reality to be experienced.

Paul writes, *"The Spirit Himself bears witness with our spirit that we are children of God"* (Romans 8:16, NKJV). This witness is not emotional hype or fleeting feeling. It is quiet assurance. It is the inward confidence that God is not against you, not distant, and not waiting for you to fail.

When this witness is ignored or underdeveloped, believers may know sonship intellectually while living uncertain emotionally. They may affirm truth outwardly while inwardly feeling unsteady. Sonship consciousness settles the heart. It anchors the soul in belonging rather than performance.

For some believers, sonship language feels unfamiliar or even uncomfortable. Not because it is unbiblical, but because it confronts years of fear-based thinking. Many learned how to relate to authority through experiences that were harsh, inconsistent, or distant. Without realizing it, they project those expectations onto God. Jesus addressed this distortion when He said, *"If you then, being evil, know how to give good gifts to your children, how much more will your heavenly Father give the Holy Spirit to those who ask Him"* (Luke 11:13, NKJV). God is not a perfected version of your past authority figures. He is a good Father.

Sonship consciousness often requires relearning how to relate to God. It involves allowing Scripture to redefine expectations and letting the Spirit heal distorted perceptions of authority and care.

Rest, Access, and Inheritance

Throughout His ministry, Jesus consistently withdrew to pray. Not because He was unsure of His standing, but because intimacy sustained His assignment. He said, *"The Son can do nothing of Himself, but what He sees the Father do"* (John 5:19, NKJV). This statement reveals dependence, not insecurity. Jesus was not afraid of acting independently. He was anchored in relationship. Slavery thinking pushes people to act from pressure. Sonship allows rest to guide action.

One concern often raised about sonship teaching is that it might produce pride. Scripture shows the opposite. **True sonship produces humility because it is rooted in grace, not entitlement.** Paul reminds us, *"By grace you have been saved through faith… it is the gift of God"* (Ephesians 2:8, NKJV). Sons know they did not earn their place. That awareness keeps the heart soft and teachable. Confidence rooted in grace does not boast. It rests.

Sonship also produces bold access to God. *"Let us therefore come boldly to the throne of grace"* (Hebrews 4:16, NKJV). This boldness is not irreverence. It is freedom from fear. Sons do not schedule appointments to ask for help. They come freely. Access is not earned through behavior. It is granted through relationship.

Correction itself is transformed under sonship. Slavery thinking sees correction as rejection. Sonship sees correction as love. *"For whom the Lord loves He chastens"* (Hebrews 12:6, NKJV). Correction is not evidence of distance. It is proof of belonging.

Paul connects sonship directly to inheritance when he writes, *"If children, then heirs"* (Romans 8:17, NKJV). Inheritance flows naturally from identity. Authority grows from belonging. Dominion is exercised most confidently by those who know where they stand. You cannot confidently possess what you secretly feel unworthy to receive.

So ask yourself honestly. Do you see God primarily as your Father or as your Judge? Do you approach Him with confidence or caution? Do you feel at home in His presence or perpetually on edge?

These questions are not meant to condemn. They are meant to restore.

Sonship is not something you strive to become. It is something you learn to rest in. *"You are no longer a slave but a son"* (Galatians 4:7, NKJV). That is not a goal. It is a declaration.

As sonship consciousness settles, fear loosens its grip. Confidence grows quietly. Faith becomes relational rather than mechanical.

In the next chapter, we will explore **Covenant Thinking**, and how sons learn to think in terms of rights, access, and responsibility without slipping back into performance.

For now, let this truth anchor your heart:
You are not trying to earn your place.
You are learning how to live from it.

CHAPTER FIVE

COVENANT THINKING

Sonship tells you who you are. Covenant thinking teaches you how God relates to you. Many believers have come to accept that they are children of God, yet they still live uncertain about what that relationship truly means in daily life. They believe God loves them, but they are unsure what that love obligates Him to do. They trust His character in principle, yet hesitate when it comes to expectation. Faith feels sincere but fragile. Prayer feels reverent but cautious. Confidence rises and falls with circumstances rather than resting in assurance.

That hesitation is often mislabeled as humility. In reality, it is usually the absence of covenant understanding. Christianity is not built on goodwill alone. It is built on covenant. God does not relate to His people through vague kindness or emotional intention. He binds Himself by His Word. Until believers learn to think covenantally, faith will remain unstable, prayer will feel uncertain, and confidence will be shaped more by experience than by truth.

From the beginning of Scripture, God reveals Himself as a covenant-making and covenant-keeping God. He does not speak casually, and He does not promise loosely. When God speaks, He commits. He said to Noah, *"I establish My covenant with you"* (Genesis 9:11, NKJV). He said to Abraham, *"I will establish My covenant between Me and you… to be God to you"* (Genesis 17:7, NKJV). He said to Israel, *"If you will indeed obey My voice and keep My covenant, then you shall be a special treasure to Me"* (Exodus 19:5, NKJV). In every instance, God did not say "I might." He said, "I will."

Covenant thinking begins when believers understand that God's promises are not expressions of goodwill. They are expressions of commitment. **God places His integrity, His name, and His reputation behind His Word.** The psalmist declared, *"He has remembered His covenant forever, the word which He commanded, for a thousand* *generations"* (Psalm 105:8, NKJV). Time does not weaken God's Word. Delay does not dilute His commitment. Circumstances do not cancel covenant. When God speaks, He commits Himself fully.

Covenant Versus Fear-Based Faith

A promise can be withdrawn. A covenant binds the one who makes it. This is why slavery thinking struggles with covenant understanding. Covenant invites expectation, and expectation feels dangerous to a mind shaped by fear. Slavery thinking avoids hope in order to avoid disappointment. It manages expectations to protect itself from pain. It says quietly, "I don't want to assume," or "I don't want to be disappointed," or "I'll believe it when I see it." What sounds cautious is often fear disguised as wisdom.

Covenant thinking speaks differently. It says, "God has spoken." It says, "God has committed Himself." It says, "I can stand on His Word." David understood this when he declared, *"The Lord is my shepherd; I shall not want"* (Psalm 23:1, NKJV). That statement was not optimism or emotional confidence. It was covenant assurance. David was not presuming provision. He was trusting the nature of his covenant Partner.

One of the greatest errors believers make is anchoring faith in outcomes rather than in God's character. Covenant thinking reverses that. Paul writes, *"If we are faithless, He remains faithful; He cannot deny Himself"* (2 Timothy 2:13, NKJV). God's faithfulness is not dependent on our consistency. It is rooted in who He is. Scripture ties God's promises directly to His name, declaring, *"You have magnified Your word above all Your name"* (Psalm 138:2, NKJV). God protects His Word because His name is attached to it.

When covenant understanding is absent, faith becomes emotional. It rises when circumstances are favorable and collapses when pressure appears. But covenant thinking produces stability. Hebrews exhorts believers to *"hold fast the confession of our hope without wavering, for He who promised is faithful"* (Hebrews 10:23, NKJV). The reason given for steadfastness is not personal discipline or emotional strength. It is God's faithfulness. Covenant thinking allows believers to remain steady even when feelings fluctuate.

Living From the Covenant Christ Established

The ultimate expression of covenant is found in Jesus Christ. Scripture declares that He is the Mediator of *"a better covenant, which was established on better promises"* (Hebrews 8:6, NKJV). This covenant is not based on human performance. It is grounded entirely in Christ's finished work. Jesus said, *"This cup is the new covenant in My blood, which is shed for you"* (Luke 22:20, NKJV). The blood of Jesus is the seal of the covenant. It speaks permanently. It does not fade with time, weaken under pressure, or fail in adversity.

Covenant thinking rests in what Christ has already done, not in what we are trying to achieve. This changes how believers pray. Without covenant understanding, prayer often feels cautious and repetitive, as though access must be negotiated. But Scripture invites believers to *"come boldly to the throne of grace"* (Hebrews 4:16, NKJV). This boldness is not irreverence. It is covenant confidence. Jesus taught His disciples to pray, *"Your will be done on earth as it is in heaven"* (Matthew 6:10, NKJV). That is covenant language. It assumes alignment between heaven and earth and expects God's will to manifest.

Covenant does not remove responsibility. It clarifies it. Paul reminds believers, *"We are His workmanship, created in Christ Jesus for good works"* (Ephesians 2:10, NKJV). Obedience flows from relationship, not fear. Sons honor covenant because they trust the One who established it. And where covenant understanding grows, peace follows. Isaiah wrote, *"You will keep him in perfect peace, whose mind is stayed on You, because he trusts in You"* (Isaiah 26:3, NKJV). Trust deepens where confidence in God's commitment is strong, and anxiety loses its grip.

So let me ask you gently. When you pray, are you hoping God will act, or resting in the confidence that He is faithful? Do you see His promises as possibilities, or as commitments sealed by covenant? Do you manage expectations, or stand on His Word?

Covenant thinking prepares the heart for expectation. Not presumption. Not entitlement. But confident anticipation rooted in God's faithfulness. In the next chapter, we will explore **Expectation as a Spiritual Law**, and how covenant understanding fuels expectation without slipping back into fear-based faith. For now, let this truth anchor your heart:

The covenant-keeping God has committed Himself to His Word.

You are not negotiating with a stranger.
You are standing with a covenant Partner.

CHAPTER SIX

EXPECTATION AS A SPIRITUAL LAW

Expectation is not optimism. It is not wishful thinking or emotional excitement. Expectation is a spiritual posture shaped by truth. Many believers misunderstand expectation because they confuse it with emotion. They assume expectation means feeling confident all the time or maintaining constant enthusiasm. But biblical expectation runs much deeper than feelings. It is a settled posture of the heart that flows naturally from covenant understanding and sonship identity. Expectation is how faith looks when it has matured.

Faith does not operate in a vacuum. It functions within an atmosphere, and that atmosphere is expectation. The writer of Hebrews defines faith as *"the substance of things hoped for, the evidence of things not seen"* (Hebrews 11:1, NKJV). The word "hoped" does not refer to uncertain longing. It speaks of confident expectation. Faith gives substance to what the heart already anticipates. Where expectation is absent, faith struggles to take shape. This explains why many believers sincerely affirm the truth of God's Word yet struggle to see fruit. Their theology may be sound, but their expectation has been trained downward by disappointment, fear, or prolonged waiting.

Expectation Must Be Trained, Not Assumed

Expectation does not develop automatically. It must be cultivated. No one begins the Christian life with healthy expectation. Expectation is shaped over time by experience, teaching, and interpretation of circumstances. Scripture acknowledges this reality when it says, *"Hope deferred makes the heart sick"* (Proverbs 13:12, NKJV). When hope is repeatedly deferred without understanding, the heart learns to lower expectation as a defense mechanism. This is not rebellion. It is self-protection.

Yet Scripture never instructs believers to reduce expectation. Instead, it teaches them to anchor it correctly. Biblical expectation is not anchored in outcomes. It is anchored in God's character. The psalmist declared, *"I wait for the Lord, my soul waits, and in His word I do hope"* (Psalm 130:5, NKJV). When the Word stops shaping expectation, life takes over. That is how disappointment becomes doctrine. But God Himself declares, *"My word… shall not return to Me void"* (Isaiah 55:11, NKJV). Expectation grows where trust in God's Word is restored.

Expectation Prepares the Ground for Faith

Expectation and faith are partners. Expectation prepares the ground. Faith acts upon it. Jesus often addressed expectation before releasing power. When blind Bartimaeus cried out, Jesus asked him, *"What do you want Me to do for you?"* (Mark 10:51, NKJV). The question was not informational. It was invitational. It was designed to awaken expectation.

In contrast, when Jesus returned to His hometown, Scripture tells us that *"He did not do many mighty works there because of their unbelief"* (Matthew 13:58, NKJV). That unbelief was not hostility. It was familiarity without expectation. Expectation determines receptivity. Where expectation is weak, faith finds little room to operate.

Expectation is Not Presumption

Scripture carefully distinguishes expectation from presumption. Presumption demands. Expectation trusts. Presumption says, "God must." Expectation says, "God is faithful." The psalmist captured this posture when he wrote, *"My expectation is from Him"* (Psalm 62:5, NKJV). Expectation that flows from God produces peace, not pressure. It rests rather than strains.

Expectation is deeply shaped by sonship. Slavery thinking avoids expectation because it fears disappointment. Sonship embraces expectation because it trusts the Father's heart. Jesus said, *"If you then, being evil, know how to give good gifts… how much more will your Father in heaven"* (Matthew 7:11, NKJV). Where God's goodness is trusted, expectation grows. Where it is questioned, expectation shrinks.

Expectation Requires Endurance and Protection

Biblical expectation is patient, not passive. Hebrews exhorts believers not to cast away their confidence, reminding them that endurance is required to receive what has been promised (Hebrews 10:35–36, NKJV). Expectation does not mean instant fulfillment. It means sustained confidence while waiting. Abraham is described as one who, *"contrary to hope, in hope believed"* (Romans 4:18, NKJV). He did not deny reality. He refused to let reality dictate expectation.

Expectation also produces emotional stability. Isaiah writes, *"You will keep him in perfect peace, whose mind is stayed on You"* (Isaiah 26:3, NKJV). When expectation is anchored in God, anxiety loses its authority. Challenges remain, but they no longer rule the heart.

Expectation is vulnerable, it must be guarded. Solomon warns, *"Guard your heart with all diligence"* (Proverbs 4:23, NKJV). Cynicism, bitterness, and unbelief slowly erode expectation if left unchecked. That is why expectation is not naive. It is disciplined.

Expectation ultimately shapes speech. Paul writes, *"I believed and therefore I spoke"* (2 Corinthians 4:13, NKJV). Words reveal expectation. They either reinforce hope or undermine it.

So pause and ask yourself honestly. What do you expect when you pray? What do you anticipate when you obey? What story do you tell yourself while waiting? Your answers reveal whether expectation is active or suppressed.

Expectation is not the final destination. It is the bridge between covenant and action. In the next chapter, we will explore **Confidence Without Arrogance**, and how expectation matures into boldness that honors God and blesses others without drifting into pride.

For now, let this truth settle in your heart:

"Blessed is the man who trusts in the Lord, and whose hope is the Lord" (Jeremiah 17:7, NKJV).

Expectation anchored in God will never leave you empty.

CHAPTER SEVEN

CONFIDENCE WITHOUT ARROGANCE

One of the greatest tensions believers face as they grow in faith is learning how to walk confidently without becoming proud. For many, confidence feels dangerous. Boldness is easily mistaken for arrogance, and authority is often confused with rebellion. As a result, believers choose caution over courage and restraint over faith. They soften conviction, delay obedience, and shrink their voice in the name of humility.

This fear has silenced more believers than failure ever did.

God never intended confidence to be threatening. He intended it to be normal. The problem is not confidence itself. The problem is the source from which confidence flows. Confidence that rises from self will always drift toward pride. But confidence that flows from sonship settles into humility without shrinking.

Arrogance is self-centered confidence. Biblical confidence is God-centered assurance. Arrogance draws attention to self. Confidence rooted in sonship points back to God. Paul articulated this distinction clearly when he wrote, *"Not that we are sufficient of ourselves to think of anything as being from ourselves, but our sufficiency is from God"* (2 Corinthians 3:5, NKJV). That statement is not insecurity. It is clarity. True confidence does not deny weakness. It simply refuses to let weakness define identity.

Humility, Grace, and Secure Identity

For many believers, confidence feels unsafe because they were taught that humility means invisibility. Strength was something to be hidden. Conviction was something to soften. Bold faith was treated as pride. But Scripture never defines humility as self-erasure. Paul exhorted believers, *"Let nothing be done through selfish ambition or conceit, but in lowliness of mind let each esteem others better than himself"* (Philippians 2:3, NKJV). Humility is not thinking less of yourself. It is thinking of yourself less.

Jesus embodied this balance perfectly. He walked with unmistakable authority, spoke plainly, and confronted error without hesitation, yet He was never arrogant. Scripture says He taught *"as one having authority, and not as the scribes"* (Matthew 7:29, NKJV). His authority flowed from intimacy with the Father, not insecurity. When challenged, He did not defend Himself anxiously. When praised, He redirected glory. His confidence was quiet, not loud. Settled, not defensive.

This kind of confidence is the fruit of grace. Paul testified, *"By the grace of God I am what I am… yet not I, but the grace of God which was with me"* (1 Corinthians 15:10, NKJV). Grace did not make Paul timid. It made him effective. Grace removes the need to strive for validation, allowing confidence to grow without arrogance.

Sonship Produces Calm Authority

Arrogance is often misunderstood as strength, but Scripture reveals it as insecurity wearing armor. Pride compensates for uncertainty. It boasts because it lacks rest. *"Pride goes before destruction"* (Proverbs 16:18, NKJV) because it elevates self in the absence of trust. Confidence, by contrast, rests because it knows who God is.

When sonship is settled, confidence no longer feels risky. Paul writes, *"You are all sons of God through faith in Christ Jesus"* (Galatians 3:26, NKJV). Secure believers are no longer trying to prove worth. They are responding from belonging. They do not dominate conversations or impress God. They are comfortable standing quietly in truth.

This security reshapes prayer. Confidence rooted in sonship shifts prayer from pleading to agreement. John writes, *"This is the confidence that we have in Him, that if we ask anything according to His will, He hears us"* (1 John 5:14, NKJV). Confidence here is not entitlement. It is alignment. The believer is not forcing God's hand. They are trusting God's heart.

Living Confidently Without Compromise

Biblical confidence expresses itself quietly in daily life. It appears in obedience without fear, decision-making without panic, waiting without anxiety, and correction without collapse. Paul encouraged

Timothy, *"Let no one despise your youth, but be an example to the believers"* (1 Timothy 4:12, NKJV). Confidence does not demand respect. It lives in such a way that respect follows.

Many believers compromise not because they want to sin, but because they lack confidence. They doubt their discernment. They fear being wrong. James warns, *"A double-minded man is unstable in all his ways"* (James 1:8, NKJV). Confidence rooted in truth produces stability. It allows believers to stand firm without becoming rigid and to speak clearly without becoming harsh.

Let me ask you honestly. Do you shrink back kwhen God calls you forward? Do you soften conviction to stay comfortable? Do you confuse bold faith with pride? If so, this chapter is not correcting you. It is releasing you. God is not threatened by your confidence. He is glorified by it.

Confidence is not the end of the journey. It is preparation. In the next chapter, we will explore **Faith That Speaks First**, and how mature confidence finds expression through aligned speech rather than impulsive words.

For now, let this truth settle in your heart:

"The righteous are bold as a lion" (Proverbs 28:1, NKJV).

Boldness rooted in righteousness is not arrogance. It is obedience.

CHAPTER EIGHT

FAITH THAT SPEAKS FIRST

Faith does not begin with action. It begins with agreement. Before faith moves your feet, it shapes your mouth. Before it confronts resistance, it settles conviction. Before it changes circumstances, it establishes language. This is why Scripture gives so much attention to speech. Words are not an afterthought in the life of faith. They are often the first evidence of what the heart truly believes.

Many believers struggle not because they lack faith, but because they have never learned how faith speaks. They believe the Word of God is true, yet their words consistently echo fear, caution, or resignation. They trust God in their hearts, yet their mouths betray hesitation. Faith that does not speak eventually weakens. Faith that speaks wrongly eventually contradicts itself. This chapter is not about positive talk or verbal optimism. It is about alignment. It is about learning to let faith take the lead in speech, especially before circumstances change.

God Speaks Before He Acts

From the opening pages of Scripture, we see a consistent divine pattern. God speaks before He acts. *"Then God said, 'Let there be light'; and there was light"* (Genesis 1:3, NKJV). Creation did not begin with movement. It began with speech. God did not wait to see light before declaring it. He spoke first, and reality followed. This reveals something essential about how God operates. Words are not reactions. They are instruments.

Faith that reflects God's nature does the same. Faith does not wait for permission from circumstances. It speaks from agreement with truth. Paul makes this connection explicit when he writes, *"I believed and therefore I spoke"* (2 Corinthians 4:13, NKJV). Belief comes first, but speech follows naturally. Speech is not optional. It is the expression of faith. Faith that never finds voice is often faith that never matures.

Why Faith Often Waits to Speak

Many believers have been trained, consciously or unconsciously, to speak last rather than first. They wait for evidence. They wait for improvement. They wait for certainty. They say things like, "Let's see how it goes," or "I'm just being realistic," or "I don't want to say too much." These statements sound wise, but they are often rooted in fear rather than discernment.

Slavery thinking waits for permission. Sonship speaks from alignment. Faith does not deny reality. It refuses to be ruled by it. Scripture makes this clear when it declares, *"Death and life are in the power of the tongue"* (Proverbs 18:21, NKJV). Words do not influence life occasionally. They carry authority. What you consistently say eventually shapes what you expect. And what you expect shapes how you live.

Speaking in Agreement With God

Faith does not speak recklessly. It speaks in agreement. The psalmist declared, *"Let the redeemed of the Lord say so"* (Psalm 107:2, NKJV). Redemption is declared, not whispered. Agreement with God is voiced. Faith does not invent reality.

It aligns with truth. This is why speaking Scripture matters, not as ritual or formula, but as alignment. When believers speak God's Word, they are not trying to convince God. They are aligning their hearts, minds, and environments with heaven's verdict.

Jesus modeled this consistently. Standing before Lazarus' tomb, with death still evident and the stone still in place, Jesus did not wait for change before speaking. He said, *"Father, I thank You that You have heard Me"* (John 11:41, NKJV). Gratitude came before resurrection. He spoke from relationship, not from evidence. When Jesus addressed the fig tree, nothing appeared to happen immediately. Yet His words preceded the manifestation. By the next day, the tree had withered from the roots (Mark 11:14, 20).

Jesus later explained this principle plainly, teaching that faith speaks to mountains before they move (Mark 11:22–23). Faith that speaks first is not reckless. It is relational.

When Silence Becomes Agreement With Fear

Silence is not always wisdom. There are moments when silence reflects trust. But there are other moments when silence becomes agreement with fear. When God has spoken, silence can become disobedience. Jeremiah captured this tension when he wrote that God's Word burned within him until he could no longer remain quiet (Jeremiah 20:9). Faith that has truly received God's Word struggles to stay silent.

There are seasons when God is waiting for agreement from your mouth, not more prayer from your heart. Words do not only affect external circumstances. They shape the inner world of the speaker. David understood this when he spoke to his own soul, commanding it to hope in God (Psalm 42:5). He did not wait for emotions to change. He spoke truth to them.

Faith speaks to fear. It speaks to doubt. It speaks to discouragement. As believers consistently speak in alignment with God's Word, the inner world begins to reorder itself around truth.

Speech Reveals the Heart

Jesus said plainly, *"Out of the abundance of the heart the mouth speaks"* (Matthew 12:34, NKJV). Speech reveals what has been stored internally. That is why careless words matter. They expose belief systems that need healing. James warns believers about inconsistent speech, noting that blessing and cursing from the same mouth reflect inner conflict, not spiritual failure (James 3:10). Faith that speaks first does not deny reality. It acknowledges pressure without surrendering to despair. Paul modeled this balance when he wrote, *"We are hard-pressed on every side, yet not crushed"* (2 Corinthians 4:8, NKJV).

Faith names the problem without enthroning it. It speaks truth over facts, not instead of them.

Speaking Well in Waiting Seasons

Waiting seasons test speech. When answers delay, words reveal what the heart is anchored to. Complaining, murmuring, and resignation often surface in seasons of delay. Israel's wilderness journey illustrates this clearly. Though God delivered them powerfully, their words consistently undermined their progress (1 Corinthians 10:10). Their words did not change God's faithfulness. They revealed unbelief that limited movement.

Faith that speaks first guards its language during waiting. One of the most practical expressions of this is intentional blessing. God instructed Moses to bless the people by speaking God's name over them (Numbers 6:27). Blessing is spoken. Identity is affirmed through words. Parents bless children. Leaders bless people. Believers bless their own lives when they speak God's promises over themselves. This is not arrogance. It is obedience.

A Pastoral Pause

Let me ask you honestly. What do you say when pressure rises? What do you speak when prayer feels unanswered? What language dominates your waiting seasons? Your words are not casual. They are formative. Faith that speaks first does not guarantee instant results, but it does guarantee alignment.

Faith that speaks first is not loud. It is consistent. It does not shout to convince others. It speaks to remain aligned. Paul exhorted believers to let their speech be gracious and seasoned with wisdom (Colossians 4:6). Faith-filled speech strengthens rather than pressures. It builds rather than performs.

This chapter prepares us for the final movements of this journey. Faith that speaks first sets the stage for peace, endurance, and daily living from inheritance.

In the next chapter, we will explore **Peace as Proof of Trust**, and how inner rest becomes evidence that faith is anchored and expectation is healthy.

For now, let this truth settle deeply in your heart:

"I believed, and therefore I spoke."
Faith that speaks first is not reckless.
It is responsive.

CHAPTER NINE

PEACE AS PROOF OF TRUST

One of the clearest indicators that faith has moved from theory into maturity is peace. Not the kind of peace that comes when everything is resolved, but the kind that remains when questions are unanswered, timelines are unclear, and outcomes are still unfolding. Peace, in this sense, is not an emotion you manufacture. It is evidence that trust has taken root in the heart.

Many believers assume that strong faith must always look intense. They associate faith with urgency, pressure, and constant motion. But Scripture reveals a different picture. Mature faith often carries a quiet confidence. It does not rush. It does not panic. It does not need to announce itself. Peace is what faith looks like when it has stopped striving to control what only God can govern.

This chapter is not about avoiding responsibility or minimizing challenges. It is about learning to recognize peace as a spiritual signal. Where peace is present, trust is active. Where peace is consistently absent, trust may still be forming.

Peace Is Not the Absence of Trouble

Biblical peace does not mean that everything around you is calm. It means that something within you is anchored. Jesus made this distinction clear when He said, *"Peace I leave with you, My peace I give to you; not as the world gives do I give to you"* (John 14:27, NKJV). The peace Jesus gives does not depend on favorable conditions. It comes from relationship.

The world's peace is fragile because it is circumstantial. When situations change, peace evaporates. But the peace Christ gives is rooted in His presence and authority. It remains even when circumstances are unresolved. That is why Jesus could promise peace to His disciples on the eve of betrayal, suffering, and separation. He was not promising comfort. He was imparting stability.

This kind of peace does not deny reality. It coexists with pressure, grief, and uncertainty. But it refuses to let those things dominate the inner life.

Anxiety as a Diagnostic Tool

Scripture does not shame anxiety. It reveals it. When Paul wrote, *"Be anxious for nothing"* (Philippians 4:6, NKJV), he was not condemning emotional struggle. He was offering direction. Anxiety, in biblical terms, is not proof of failure. It is an invitation to re-anchor trust.

Anxiety surfaces when the heart begins to carry weight it was never meant to hold. It grows when outcomes feel personal, when control feels necessary, and when trust feels risky. In those moments, the heart tightens, thoughts accelerate, and peace recedes.

Paul does not tell believers to suppress anxiety. He tells them to redirect it. Through prayer, thanksgiving, and surrender, anxiety becomes a signal that it is time to place something back into God's hands.

Peace as a Guard, Not a Passive State

Paul describes peace as an active force when he writes, *"The peace of God… will guard your hearts and minds through Christ Jesus"* (Philippians 4:7, NKJV). Peace does not sit quietly on the sidelines. It stands watch. It protects the inner life from fear-driven thinking, emotional overload, and impulsive reactions.

Where peace is allowed to rule, the heart remains steady even under pressure. Where peace is ignored, the mind becomes vulnerable to speculation, worst-case scenarios, and spiritual exhaustion. Peace functions like a boundary. It keeps the heart from wandering into fear-filled territory.

This is why peace is such a valuable indicator of spiritual health. It reveals whether the heart is trusting God or trying to manage outcomes alone.

Jesus and the Power of Restful Trust

One of the most striking images of peace in the Gospels is Jesus asleep in the boat during a storm. While experienced fishermen panicked, Scripture tells us that Jesus was sleeping (Mark 4:38). His rest was not carelessness. It was confidence.

When the disciples woke Him in fear, Jesus did not immediately address the storm. He addressed their hearts. *"Why are you so fearful?"* He asked (Mark 4:40, NKJV). His question reveals something profound. The presence of danger did not trouble Him. The presence of fear did.

Peace is not ignorance of danger. It is trust in authority. Jesus rested because He knew who was with Him, where He was going, and whose hands governed the outcome.

Peace and the Test of Time

Waiting is one of the greatest tests of peace. When answers delay, peace is often the first thing challenged. The psalmist understood this when he wrote, *"Rest in the Lord, and wait patiently for Him"* (Psalm 37:7, NKJV). Waiting without peace becomes torment. Waiting with peace becomes formation.

Delay does not threaten trust when peace is present. Instead, it deepens dependence. Peace during waiting says, "God is at work even when I cannot see progress." It resists the urge to rush solutions or force outcomes.

Many believers lose peace not because God is absent, but because timing feels uncomfortable. Yet Scripture consistently shows that God uses waiting seasons to mature trust.

Peace Protects Against Compromise

A restless heart is more likely to compromise. When peace is absent, decisions are rushed. Shortcuts are tempting. Discernment becomes clouded. James warns that where confusion reigns, destructive patterns often follow (James 3:16).

Peace brings clarity. It slows the heart enough to listen. It allows wisdom to surface. It creates space for discernment. A peaceful heart is far less vulnerable to pressure-driven choices.

This is why Scripture instructs believers to let peace rule their hearts (Colossians 3:15). Peace becomes an internal referee, signaling when alignment is present and when caution is needed.

Trust and Peace Are Intertwined

Trust and peace grow together. As trust deepens, peace increases. As peace strengthens, trust becomes more evident. Solomon captured this connection when he wrote, *"Trust in the Lord with all your heart... and He shall direct your paths"* (Proverbs 3:5–6, NKJV).

Peace does not mean understanding everything. It means trusting God even when understanding is incomplete. It is the quiet assurance that God sees what you cannot see and is handling what you cannot control.

Peace in the Midst of Spiritual Resistance

Peace does not disappear when spiritual resistance arises. In fact, it becomes one of the believer's greatest defenses. Paul includes peace as part of the armor of God, calling it *"the preparation of the gospel of peace"* (Ephesians 6:15, NKJV). Peace stabilizes the believer's stance.

A believer grounded in peace is difficult to intimidate. Fear loses leverage. Pressure loses urgency. The enemy thrives on agitation, but peace resists manipulation.

Peace as a Mark of Maturity

Immature faith reacts quickly. Mature faith responds calmly. Paul encouraged believers to let gentleness be evident (Philippians 4:5). Gentleness is not weakness. It is strength under control.

Peace reflects confidence in God's sovereignty. It shows that the believer is no longer trying to prove faith, but is learning to live from it.

A Gentle Moment of Self-Examination

Take a moment to reflect honestly. How do you respond when answers delay? What happens inside you when situations feel uncertain? Does peace return quickly, or does anxiety linger?

These questions are not accusations. They are invitations. Peace develops gradually as trust is practiced consistently.

Cultivating Peace Intentionally

Peace is strengthened through intentional habits. Renewing the mind with Scripture stabilizes thought patterns. Prayer releases pressure. Thanksgiving redirects focus. Guarding influences protects emotional health.

Paul emphasized thanksgiving because gratitude anchors the heart in trust. *"In everything give thanks"* (1 Thessalonians 5:18, NKJV). Gratitude and peace reinforce one another.

Peace as a Living Testimony

Peace speaks louder than words. When others panic and you remain steady, peace testifies. When outcomes are uncertain and you rest, peace testifies. It reveals a confidence that cannot be explained by circumstances alone.

Peter encourages believers to be ready to explain their hope (1 Peter 3:15). Often, peace is what prompts the question.

Preparing for Everyday Living

This chapter marks a turning point. Peace confirms that slavery thinking has loosened its grip. It signals readiness to live daily from inheritance rather than fear.

In the next and final chapter, we will bring everything together by exploring **Thinking Like an Heir Every Day**. This is where theology becomes lifestyle and revelation becomes rhythm.

For now, let this truth settle deeply:

"Now may the Lord of peace Himself give you peace always in every way" (2 Thessalonians 3:16, NKJV).

Peace is not the absence of faith.
It is the evidence that trust has matured.

CHAPTER TEN

THINKING LIKE AN HEIR EVERY DAY

Inheritance is not activated in moments. It is expressed in patterns.

Many believers encounter powerful truths about identity, authority, and inheritance, yet struggle to sustain them in everyday life. Revelation often comes quickly, but transformation unfolds slowly. It is one thing to understand sonship in prayer or teaching, and another thing to carry that mindset into ordinary routines, difficult conversations, financial pressure, relational tension, and long seasons where nothing dramatic seems to be happening.

This is where many believers unintentionally drift. They do not reject truth. They simply fail to

practice it consistently. Old habits of thinking quietly resurface. Fear regains a voice. Scarcity whispers again. Control tightens subtly. The mind, left unattended, often returns to what is familiar rather than what is true.

That is why inheritance must become a **daily way of thinking**, not an occasional spiritual realization. Heirship is sustained in the mundane. It is proven in repetition. It is revealed in how you interpret life when no one is watching and nothing feels urgent.

Thinking like an heir is not a spiritual event. It is a disciplined posture learned over time.

Heirs Live From Provision, Not Panic

One of the clearest distinctions between slave thinking and heir thinking is how needs are approached. A slave mentality responds to need with panic, anxiety, and urgency. It immediately asks, "What if this doesn't work?" or "What happens if God doesn't come through this time?" These questions may feel practical, but they are rooted in insecurity rather than wisdom.

Heirs, on the other hand, approach needs from relationship. They acknowledge reality without surrendering to fear. They plan responsibly without allowing anxiety to govern decisions. This posture flows directly from Jesus' teaching when He said, *"Your heavenly Father knows that you need all these things"* (Matthew 6:32, NKJV). That statement reframes everything. It does not deny need. It affirms care.

Heir thinking does not eliminate effort. It eliminates panic. It replaces frantic striving with confident dependence. When provision feels threatened, heirs return to identity rather than fear. They remind themselves not only of what they need, but of **who their Father is**.

Daily heir thinking asks, "How does trust respond here?" instead of, "How do I control this?"

Heirs Interpret Delays Through Trust, Not Accusation

Delay is one of the greatest tests of mindset. To a slave mentality, delay feels personal. It feels like rejection, punishment, or failure. The mind begins to ask accusatory questions: "Did I miss God?" "Am I unqualified?" "Is this ever going to happen?"

Heir thinking responds differently. It does not romanticize waiting, but it does not internalize delay as condemnation. Scripture reminds us, *"Though it tarries, wait for it"* (Habakkuk 2:3, NKJV). That instruction assumes trust. It assumes that timing serves purpose, even when purpose is not immediately visible.

Heirs learn that God's silence is not absence and His delay is not denial. They resist the urge to rush outcomes simply to relieve discomfort. Instead, they allow waiting to refine patience, strengthen character, and deepen dependence.

Daily heir thinking refuses to let delay rewrite identity.

Heirs Make Decisions From Identity, Not Fear

Many believers make decisions primarily to avoid loss, discomfort, or uncertainty. Fear becomes the silent advisor. Choices are made quickly, not because clarity is present, but because tension feels unbearable.

Heir thinking slows the process. Scripture says, *"As many as are led by the Spirit of God, these are sons of God"* (Romans 8:14, NKJV). Sons and daughters are led, not driven. Heirs are not pressured into movement by anxiety. They wait for alignment.

This does not mean indecision or passivity. It means discernment. Heirs value peace as guidance. They listen inwardly. They recognize when urgency is emotional rather than spiritual.

Daily heir thinking asks, "Does this decision agree with who I am in Christ?" rather than, "How fast can I make this discomfort go away?"

Heirs Respond to Failure Without Shame

Failure exposes mindset quickly. Slavery thinking collapses under failure. It internalizes shame and assumes disqualification. The inner voice becomes harsh, condemning, and final.

Heir thinking responds with humility and confidence simultaneously. Scripture assures us, *"If anyone sins, we have an Advocate with the Father"* (1 John 2:1, NKJV). Advocacy assumes relationship. Correction assumes belonging.

Heirs repent quickly because they feel safe. They do not hide from God. They return to Him. Failure becomes a place of refinement, not rejection. Daily heir thinking separates identity from performance. It refuses to let a moment define a life.

Heirs Speak Differently to Themselves

One of the most overlooked aspects of heirship is **inner dialogue**. What you say to yourself consistently shapes how you live. David understood this when he spoke to his own soul, saying, *"Bless the Lord, O my soul, and forget not all His benefits"* (Psalm 103:2, NKJV).

Heirs do not allow emotions to narrate reality unchecked. They acknowledge feelings without surrendering authority to them. They speak truth gently but firmly to fear, discouragement, and doubt.

Daily heir thinking involves intentional self-talk rooted in Scripture, not circumstance. It challenges lies without self-contempt. It reinforces truth without arrogance. What you rehearse inwardly will eventually manifest outwardly.

Heirs Steward Peace Intentionally

Peace does not sustain itself automatically. It must be stewarded. Scripture instructs believers to *"let the peace of God rule"* (Colossians 3:15, NKJV). Rule implies authority. Peace becomes a governing influence over pace, pressure, and priorities.

Heirs pay attention when peace is disrupted. They do not ignore unrest. They ask reflective questions. "What am I carrying that belongs to God?" "What expectation have I taken on that He never assigned?"

Daily heir thinking values rest as an act of trust, not weakness. It resists the culture of hurry and the illusion that constant motion equals faith.

Heirs Expect God's Faithfulness in Ordinary Life

Many believers expect God in crisis but forget Him in routine. Heir thinking integrates faith into daily life. Scripture says, *"In Him we live and move and have our being"* (Acts 17:28, NKJV). That includes meetings, conversations, work, and decisions.

Heirs expect wisdom for ordinary choices, favor in everyday interactions, and guidance in quiet moments. They do not reserve faith for emergencies. They live relationally aware.

Inheritance is not reserved for dramatic breakthroughs.

It is expressed in daily dependence.

Heirs Handle Authority With Responsibility

Authority is part of inheritance, but authority must be stewarded. Jesus taught that increased access brings increased responsibility (Luke 12:48). Heirs do not use authority to elevate self. They use it to serve others and honor God.

Daily heir thinking asks reflective questions before acting: "Does this build?" "Does this reflect Christ?" "Does this serve God's purpose or my ego?"

True authority is exercised with restraint, wisdom, and humility.

Heirs Refuse Comparison and Competition

Slavery thinking compares constantly. It measures worth by proximity, progress, or recognition. Heir thinking rests in assignment. Scripture reminds us that there are different gifts but the same Spirit (1 Corinthians 12:4).

Heirs celebrate others without feeling diminished. They understand that another person's success does not threaten their inheritance. They trust God's distribution. Comparison loses power when identity is settled.

Heirs Live With Generational Vision

Inheritance is not only personal. It is generational. Scripture says, *"A good man leaves an inheritance to his children's children"* (Proverbs 13:22, NKJV). Heirs think beyond themselves. They consider legacy, patterns, values, and spiritual impact.

Daily heir thinking asks, "What am I reinforcing today that will shape tomorrow?" It recognizes that habits, attitudes, and choices echo forward.

A Final Invitation to Practice

This book began by exposing slavery thinking. It ends by calling for consistency. You are not trying to become an heir. You already are one. The work now is alignment.

Paul declared, *"If children, then heirs"* (Romans 8:17, NKJV). That is settled. What remains is daily agreement.

Thinking like an heir every day is not dramatic. It is faithful. It is practiced. It is quiet. And over time, it reshapes everything.

CONCLUSION

Living From What Was Settled

This book was never about giving you something new. It was about helping you live from what was already settled.

From the beginning, the issue was never God's willingness. It was never Christ's finished work. It was never heaven's availability. The real struggle has always been internal. A struggle of mindset. A struggle of perception. A struggle between who you are and how you think.

Slavery thinking survives wherever truth is known but not embraced. It shows up when believers pray sincerely but expect little. When they obey faithfully but live cautiously. When they love God deeply but still fear disappointment. That is not rebellion. It is misalignment.

Freedom is not only something Christ gives. It is something believers must learn to walk in consciously.

Throughout this journey, you have seen that identity must be settled before confidence can grow. Covenant must move from concept to certainty. Faith must find its voice. Trust must mature into peace. And inheritance must become a daily way of thinking, not a distant hope.

The gospel does not end at forgiveness. It continues into formation.

You are not a tolerated believer trying to stay in God's favor.

You are a child learning how to live at home. That changes everything.

- You no longer interpret life through fear.
- You no longer approach God with hesitation.
- You no longer shrink back when authority is required.
- You no longer panic when timing stretches.
- You no longer measure yourself by performance.

You live anchored now.

Thinking like an heir does not make life effortless. It makes life stable. Pressure still comes, but it does not rule. Delays still happen, but they do not steal peace. Challenges still arise, but they do not define identity.

You are not preparing to inherit.
You already have.
Now live like it.

www.ingramcontent.com/pod-product-compliance
Lightning Source LLC
Chambersburg PA
CBHW070653050426
42451CB00008B/339